The People's Liberation Army

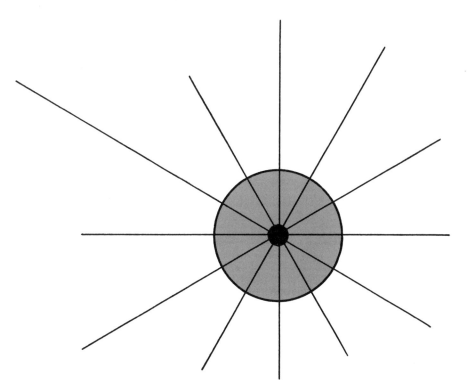

The People's Liberation Army

COMMUNIST CHINA'S ARMED FORCES

Angus M. Fraser

National Strategy Information Center, Inc.

PUBLISHED BY

Crane, Russak & Company, New York

FERNALD LIBRARY
COLBY-SAWYER COLLEGE
NEW LONDON, N. H. 03257

UA
839.3
.F7

The People's Liberation Army
Communist China's Armed Forces

Published in the United States by

Crane, Russak & Company, Inc.
52 Vanderbilt Avenue
New York, N.Y. 10017

Copyright © 1973 by
National Strategy Information Center, Inc.

No part of this publication may be reproduced,
stored in a retrieval system, or transmitted
in any form or by any means, electronic,
mechanical, photocopying, recording,
or otherwise, without the prior
written permission of the publisher.
Crane, Russak & Company, Inc.
52 Vanderbilt Avenue, New York, N.Y. 10017

Library Edition: ISBN 0-8448-0221-2

Paperbound Edition: ISBN 0-8448-0223-9

Library of Congress Catalog Card Number 73-76898

Printed in the United States of America

Strategy Papers No. 19

75426

Table of Contents

Preface

In retrospect, the bipolarity of international politics in the immediate post-World War II period had psychologically comforting aspects. The global power confrontation between Soviet Russia and the United States was understandable, and some of its manifestations predictable. One should not underestimate the dangers of that period. But given the overwhelming American superiority in SAC and strategic nuclear weapons, the threats posed by a still more or less monolithic Communist bloc seemed generally manageable. (Except, of course, for the covert challenges of ideological combat, propaganda, and political warfare, where the West has never seriously addressed the problem.)

The emergence of the People's Republic of China onto the world stage, and the subsequent split between Communist China and the Soviet Union, signaled the apparent end of bipolarity. A new, multipolar world began to take shape with, in the beginning, three main centers of power to be reckoned with—Peking in addition to Washington and Moscow. The Chinese soon developed their own nuclear capability to lend credence to their major power status. More recently, Japan's phenomenal productivity growth, and the expansion of the West European Economic Community, have brought two more economic giants (albeit still military dwarfs) into the circle of primary world decisionmakers.

Multipolarity has presented American diplomacy with new opportunities—and new dangers. One measure of the latter is the military strength of the People's Republic of China, and the extent to which the possible projections of its growing power may overshadow vital United States interests in Asia. How modern, competent, and flexible is that military capability? What does its present configuration and the main lines of its apparent development suggest with respect to Peking's foreign policy objectives? How serious a threat to American interests are the armed forces of the PRC?

These are some of the problems that Colonel A. M. Fraser deals with in the present monograph. He carefully analyzes the composition of the Chinese People's Liberation Army and Peking's various land, naval, and air components. He also describes training and equipment, in order to arrive at estimates of the present capabilities and limitations of Communist China's armed forces. He then balances these estimates against Peking's perception of contemporary threats to its own security—from the US, the USSR, and elsewhere. His main conclusion is that, however expansionist Communist China's global policy may be, Peking's primary military concern at present—reflecting its comparative military backwardness—is "defense against attack on the homeland by the United States or the Soviet Union, with a principal focus now on the latter."

Colonel Fraser retired in 1964 after a distinguished career in the US Marine Corps. While in service, he saw duty in North China immediately after World War II, and subsequently as Senior Marine Advisor, MAAG, Republic of China (Taiwan). Since retirement, Colonel Fraser has been a consultant for the Smithsonian Institute and the Historical Evaluation and Research Organization, and a staff member of the Institute for Defense Analyses. He has written and lectured widely on Asian political-military affairs.

Frank R. Barnett, *President*
National Strategy Information Center, Inc.

August 1973

1

Introduction

Mao Tse-tung teaches the Chinese nation that the People's Liberation Army is a work and propaganda force as well as a fighting force. The PLA has certainly performed in all of these roles in the evolution of the People's Republic of China. In this monograph, however, we shall put aside for a time the search for an understanding of the role of political and ideological influences in shaping Communist China's armed forces, and focus on the military characteristics and capabilities that the PLA actually appears to have today, and those it seeks in the near future. This should make it possible to reach some conclusions as to Peking's view of its present military situation, the military posture it seeks, and the impact of Chinese doctrine on the Asian strategic situation. Whatever part the foreign policy and domestic politics of the PRC may have in shaping forces, tactics, and doctrine, there is also a separate and useful core of data about the present Chinese military condition and prospects upon which an objective assessment of capabilities may be based, and from which it

1

should be possible to infer Chinese perceptions as to the main threats to its national security. This assumes, of course, that there is a logical "fit" between doctrine and forces, on the one hand, and their antici- pated employment on the other. What appears today (and what logically can be seen as likely to emerge) may not be anyone's *optimum* structure; but it does represent some consensus as to the current reality. For better or worse, this is what China has to fight with.[1]

The Chinese Communists had little leisure for the development of long-range plans or balanced programs while fighting the Japanese and Nationalist forces. Less than a year after taking over the main- land, moreover, Peking was engaged in a war in Korea whose dimen- sions and tactics it could not control. Subsequent combat experience (India, the Taiwan Strait) was limited in scope and duration; the Korean War represents the PLA's only broad educational contact with modern conventional forces. Despite its relative remoteness in time, the experience of the 1950-53 period has shaped the kinds of questions that arise in the development of doctrine and force im- provement programs. A group of eighteen captured PLA veterans were asked to assess the qualities of United Nations forces that had the greatest effect on the PLA in Korea.[2] Fourteen emphasized United Nations airpower. Their own comparative lack of mobility and fire- power came next. Other important items included the problems of operating in unfamiliar terrain; among a "different" people; lack of military training because of concentration on civilian projects; fixed fronts, lack of maneuver room, and reduction of guerrilla possibili- ties; a poor supply system and an inability to get at the United Nations lines of communication. The list reads like an Inspector General's report on a failed operation.

---

[1] The Chairman of the US Joint Chiefs of Staff has stated: "Beyond five years, it is ex- tremely difficult to say anything precise about the forces of other nations, since the data are inherently unknowable. These foreign governments, themselves, may not have made any firm decisions on force deployments even over the next five years, much less beyond that point in time." See Statement by Admiral Thomas H. Moorer, Chairman of the Joint Chiefs of Staff, February 15, 1972, in *Hearings before the Committee of Armed Services, U.S. Senate, 92nd Congress, Second Session,* Part 2 (hereafter cited as *Moorer*), p. 491.
[2] Alexander L. George, *The Chinese Communist Army in Action* (New York and London: Columbia University Press, 1967), ch. 9. While it must be kept in mind that these men were prisoners, and therefore in a sense "losers," there is a persuasive quality of realism and consistency in what they say.

If these lessons were in fact imbedded in the professional consciousness of those who went on to become planners and commanders in the PLA, it is possible to formulate a set of questions to test PLA force improvement programs against prospective force employments. Such questions might include: What has been done to increase firepower on a man and unit basis? What scale of improvement has been sought in tactical and logistical mobility? What steps have been taken to improve battlefield air defense? Has anything been done to deepen attack capabilities, and thus bring enemy bases and lines of communication under attack? What has been done to deny free use of the sea to the enemy, and to enhance the role of naval forces in support of ground operations?

These questions derive directly from the massive conventional ground nature of the Korean War. Later on, we shall have to examine the significance of nuclear weapons for the PLA, as well as the implications of war in the air and at sea.

This study seeks to isolate and describe the military characteristics and capabilities that define the operational functions of the PLA. The facts and figures used herein are drawn from a number of well-known, open sources. While sometimes contradictory, they do serve to demonstrate the upper and lower limits of what is thought about PRC armed forces and their future programs. United States Defense Department officials are quoted extensively, in the belief that they speak from knowledge and a sense of responsibility—even though they sometimes take a "worst case" approach.

2

The People's Liberation Army:
Present Position and Future Prospects

Ground Forces

An authoritative journal gives these strengths for the ground forces of the PRC:[3]

    5 armored divisions
  120 infantry divisions
    3 cavalry divisions
    2 airborne divisions
  20 artillery divisions (approximately)
Support troops—signals, engineer, railway and motor transport.
Equipment includes JS-2, T-34, and T-54 tanks (Soviet-fur-

---

[3] *The Military Balance 1972-1973* (London: International Institute for Strategic Studies, 1972) (hereafter cited as *Military Balance*), pp. 44-45.

nished); Chinese T-59 tanks (copy of Soviet T-54) and T-62 light tanks; T-60 amphibious tanks; armored personnel carriers; 152mm and 203mm artillery, and SU-76, SU-100, and JSU-122 self-propelled artillery. (Other sources relate that equipment is adequate in categories of home-produced infantry weapons, mortars, rocket-launchers, recoilless rifles, and light and medium artillery.)

This journal, for the first time, lists the PRC's Strategic Forces as follows:

IRBMs	15-20
MRBMs	20-30
Aircraft	up to 100 TU-16s

The US Secretary of Defense calls the Chinese Army a "well-balanced force containing 150 combat divisions . . . continually being modernized and upgraded."[4] Admiral Moorer has said: "The PRC Army is essentially an infantry force. Their units lack adequate organic transportation, and their inventories of fighting vehicles are still quite limited. Production of armored vehicles, artillery pieces, and all types of light infantry weapons (mostly Soviet design) has been increased significantly since 1965. It is expected that this expansion of armament production will continue in the years ahead."[5] Moorer went on to tell the Senate Committee that the PRC had a considerably greater number of artillery pieces than the United States, and that a majority of them outranged US weapons. On the other hand, US self-propelled artillery and helicopters offset the imbalance. The US, USSR, and PRC are close together in numbers of antitank weapons, but most of the PLA stock is of World War II vintage.

A less conservative view of PRC ground forces may be in order. A recent Congressional study speaks in general terms of the demonstrated ability of the PRC to develop and produce new military

---

[4] *National Security Strategy of Realistic Deterrence—Secretary of Defense Melvin R. Laird's Annual Defense Department Report Fiscal Year 1973*, February 15, 1972 (hereafter cited as *Laird*), p. 50.
[5] *Moorer*, p. 512.

hardware for its ground forces.[6] Army trucks, for example, increased by eleven percent in the last ten years; and this is reinforced by the availability of a total national truck fleet that grew from an estimated fifty thousand in 1952 to five hundred thousand in 1971. From 1950 to 1970, highways in operation rose from 99,600 km to 650,000 km; and to this must be added the constantly improving rail system (from 22,512 km in 1950 to 40,000 km in 1970) and new lines into critical strategic areas, particularly the Northwest. The improving transportation picture adds greatly to mobility and flexibility within the borders of the PRC, and makes for considerable improvement beyond them. This latter capability has been enhanced by a variety of significant roadbuilding activities, which will be discussed later.

The same study describes a healthy electronics industry, half to three quarters of whose products go to the military. The ground forces have some call on radar and computer production, but their main effort seems to look to more and better military communications. A captured man-pack patrol radio shows good quality and workmanship. Tactical communications, from army level down through platoons, were a serious weakness in the past. This has apparently been recognized.

The PRC has some additional paramilitary assets whose usefulness would vary under different conditions, but which nevertheless must be included in an assessment of total capabilities. First, there is the militia. Nelsen cites current estimates of strength ranging from thirty to a hundred million. Within these numbers, he identifies a "basic militia" of perhaps twelve to fifteen million who receive some military training for several days each year. Within *this* group (ages eighteen to forty years), there is an elite of perhaps five to seven million "armed militia"—politically screened troops who carry arms and assist in public security duties.[7] The People's Armed Police, as

[6] *People's Republic of China: An Economic Assessment* (Washington: Joint Economic Committee of the Congress, 1972) (hereafter cited as *Economic Assessment*).
[7] Harvey W. Nelsen, *An Organizational History of the Chinese People's Liberation Army 1966-1969* (Unpublished Ph.D. Dissertation) (Washington: George Washington University, 1972), p. 191.

a national force, was largely destroyed in the Cultural Revolution, and its functions absorbed by PLA units (or in some cases by locally organized and controlled provost units). Some of the core militia units could probably be found performing such duties.

Two other types of units operate on the frontiers. The pioneering effort required in a rugged area such as Sinkiang has produced a number of production and construction units, lightly armed and organized along military lines. There are also perhaps as many as twenty Border Defense and Military Internal Security divisions, armed and trained for the functions their names imply. The railway engineering divisions of the PLA also deserve special mention. There are about ten of them, trained and equipped to perform railway construction, repair, and operations tasks. At least two have seen extended service in Indochina, where they have demonstrated remarkable efficiency in putting damaged lines back into service.

Naval Forces

The standard open authority on world naval forces gives these figures for the naval component of the PLA:[8]

Submarines*	Type "G"	1
	Type "W"	21
	Type "R"	6
	Miscellaneous (smaller types)	7
Destroyers		4
Destroyer Escorts		9
Escort Vessels		11
Patrol Vessels		24
Fast Gunboats		160
Torpedo Boats (hydrofoil)		40
Torpedo Boats**		200

[8] *Jane's Fighting Ships 1971-72* (London: Jane's Yearbooks, 1971), pp. 62-67.

LST (ex-US)	16 ⎫	
LSM (ex-US)	13 ⎪	amphibious ships
LSIL (ex-US)	15 ⎬	and craft
LSU (ex-US)	10 ⎭	

* In addition to this listing, *Jane's* says that there may be up to three nuclear-powered, 3,000-ton boats under construction.
** The PRC has a significant capability for building torpedo boat types.

In addition, the Navy has smaller patrol craft, minesweepers, coastal and river defense vessels, boom vessels, and survey, repair, supply, oiler, tug, and service auxiliaries. There are also armed motor launches and motor junks. The Navy has a separate air arm, which will be discussed under Air and Air Defense Forces in the next section.

Various authorities differ somewhat as to exact numbers, particularly of submarines. *Military Balance* lists one "G" Class submarine, 32 "fleet" submarines, and three coastal types.[9] Secretary of Defense Laird spoke of "over forty" diesel-powered attack submarines.[10] The JCS Chairman gives a figure of 28 as of 1965, but cautions that the force was growing.[11] A United States naval officer has noted that the PRC has the third largest submarine fleet in the world.[12] He adds: "One need only to recall that Nazi Germany started the Second World War with a submarine fleet not much larger than China's today to appreciate its potential threat to the shipping lanes of the Pacific Ocean, which serves to transport virtually all of Japan's crude oil requirements." In fact, the Nazis actually had 57 submarines at the start of World War II. More importantly, these were World War II boats opposed by World War II antisubmarine techniques. The Chinese submarines are Soviet copies of the last German World War II types, but they are now opposed by much more sophisticated detection and destruction capabilities on the part of the United States and the Soviet Union.

---

[9] *Military Balance*, p. 45.
[10] *Laird*, p. 50.
[11] *Moorer*, p. 508.
[12] John R. Dewenter, "China Afloat," *Foreign Affairs* (July 1972).

United States military officials call attention to other aspects of PRC naval growth. According to Laird: "The Chinese Navy is concentrating on developing sophisticated weapons systems such as guided-missile destroyers and missile-equipped coastal patrol craft."[13] And Moorer: "The PRC has only lately begun to expand its fleet of major combat surface ships. Prior to 1966, this fleet consisted of eight Soviet-built ships—four destroyers and four destroyer escorts. Beginning in 1966, a new class of Chinese-built destroyer escorts was introduced and there are now a number of such ships in the fleet. In 1971, the first of a new class of Chinese guided missile destroyers was introduced, and we believe more of these ships will be built over the next several years."[14] (*Military Balance* credits the PRC navy with nine destroyer escorts and fourteen patrol escorts, a one-year increase of five and three, respectively.) Admiral Moorer went on to say: "Even though the PRC 'deep water' fleet may increase dramatically over the next several years, it will still be Asia-oriented and have only a relatively limited capability in global terms."

There seems to be a rough consensus over the size and general functional nature of PRC naval forces. Available evidence supports the general thesis of a search for improvements in quality and numbers within the framework of a generally defensive, close-in maritime posture. The submarine force does carry some offensive implications; this perspective will be put in context in a following chapter.

The PRC shipbuilding industry has been given increased support. A Chinese release suggested a rather ambitious program:[15]

> Whether or not we vigorously strive to develop the shipbuilding industry and build a powerful navy as well as a powerful maritime fleet is an important issue concerning whether or not we want to consolidate our national defense, strengthen the dictatorship of the proletariat, liberate Taiwan, and finally unify our

---

[13] *Laird*, p. 50.
[14] *Moorer*, p. 507.
[15] *People's Daily*, June 4, 1970.

motherland, develop the freight business and aquatic products enterprises, build socialism, and support world revolution.

But while the PRC's general shipbuilding capacity is growing and modernizing, it is still relatively modest. So far, the PRC has produced some diesel-powered submarines (largely from Soviet designs and components), destroyer escorts, and hydrofoil patrol craft, and a number of 10,000- to 15,000-ton cargo and tanker vessels. The PRC merchant fleet of about two hundred vessels of a thousand gross tons or over equates roughly with that of the Republic of China, and is less than five percent of the Japanese fleet. The PRC might, at some future date, embark on a "crash" program of naval construction, but as yet no evidence of this is apparent.

Air and Air Defense Forces

Military Balance gives the following particulars:[16]

	NUMBER		
TYPE	*AIR FORCE*	*NAVY*	*REMARKS*
TU-16	"about 100"		
TU-4	"a few"		
IL-28	200	100	Navy version armed with torpedos
TU-2	100		
Mig-15 } Mig-17 }	1,700	"substantial numbers"	
Mig-19	up to 1,000		
Mig-21	75		
F-9	200		
AN-2 } IL-14 } IL-18 } MI-4 (heli) }	"about 400"		Transports may be augmented by 350 civil aircraft

---

[16] *Military Balance*, p. 45.

SAM SA-2   "several hun-
                dred in up to
                fifty sites"

When placed alongside information from other sources, the figures above may seem somewhat conservative; but they nevertheless help to convey the sense of dynamism and progress that is implied in other estimates. For example, *Air Actualities*, the monthly journal of the French Air Force, reports that the PRC air force is now armed with a jet fighter, the F-9, capable of speeeds up to 1,400 miles per hour. Assembly began in April 1971; and at the time of the report, about eighty of these aircraft were believed to be in operation.[17] A later report sets the rate of production at fifteen per month, with about three hundred produced and two hundred assigned to operating squadrons.[18] Still another account says that the airplane is based on, but considerably advanced over, the Soviet Mig-19 (rated at 850 mph at 36 thousand feet). This source further stated that the combat operating radius is three hundred to five hundred miles, and service ceiling above fifty thousand feet. Production rate was thought at that time to be ten per month. A Mach-2 aircraft, designated F-9F, with advanced engine design and improved components, was also said to have gone into production.

The French Air Force journal gave the following figures on the PLA air force:

fighters	2,900
bombers	440
helicopters	300
transports	400

These were said to consist of 1,700 Mig-17s; 100 Mig-15s; 1,000 Mig-19s; 30-35 Mig-21Cs; 100 TU-2s; 300 IL-28s; and 25 TU-16s.

The Chairman of the JCS distinguished between "tactical" and "home defense" aircraft. He put six hundred in the first category and three thousand in the second, noting that some of the latter could

---

[17] *New York Times*, January 30, 1972.
[18] In *New York Times*, July 25, 1972.

be diverted to "tactical" roles.[19] It is assumed that the distinction is between attack and close support roles and the straightforward air defense of locations inside the Chinese borders.

Secretary of Defense Laird[20] estimated the PRC air force to have "over three thousand jet fighters (several hundred more than last year) and approximately 350 light and medium bombers (up by more than ten percent)." Secretary Laird reportedly told a Senate Committee in February 1970 that the PRC might have more than sixty TU-16s.[21] Murphy also reports that in March 1971, the Secretary said that the Chinese would have a significant force of TU-16s by mid-1972. Murphy estimates that the PLA air force might have somewhere between 72 and 108 of the TU-16s in service, with an end-strength in 1972 of 130 planes in four air regiments. Other analysts have taken a more conservative estimate of 30-35 TU-16s as more likely.

The PRC air defense system includes radar and surface-to-air missile components, although comparatively little is publicly known about it. It is reported to include, in addition to some three thousand aircraft, fifty SAM sites, 4,500 antiaircraft guns of various calibers, and 1,500 air defense radars.[22] The Congress was told that the "PRC will also have several hundred SAM launchers by mid-1972, and this number will probably increase gradually over the next few years."[23] The missile involved is believed to be the SU "Guideline," with a 130kg high explosive head, a slant range of forty to fifty kilometers, and a ceiling of eighteen thousand meters.[24] Of the PRC air defense system, *Military Balance* says: "There is an air defense system, initially developed to defend the eastern seaboard of China and now greatly expanded, based on early warning/control radar, interceptor aircraft, and several hundred SA-2 missiles deployed in up to fifty sites." *Strategic Survey 1971* states that a "new air defense radar was

---

[19] *Moorer*, p. 510.
[20] *Laird*, pp. 46 and 50.
[21] Charles H. Murphy, "Mainland China's Evolving Nuclear Deterrent," *Bulletin of the Atomic Scientists* (January 1972).
[22] *Jane's Weapons Systems 1972-73* (London: Jane's Yearbooks, 1972), p. 182.
[23] *Moorer*, p. 510.
[24] *Jane's Weapons Systems 1972-73*, p. 62.

seen, quite different from equipment of Soviet origin, and the Soviet-designed SAM-2 has been improved."[25]

The Chinese electronics industry is reported to be producing "early warning, ground control intercept, missile control, and naval radars; sonar, avionic equipment; missile guidance equipment; laser rangefinders; and nuclear instrumentation . . . probably also electronic countermeasures equipment, airborne radar, and infrared homing devices for missiles."[26]

As a final element in air defense, passive measures are receiving some attention. There is a continuing program for the dispersion of production facilities, with varying levels of success. A recent visitor, who toured extensively in mainland China, reports very large digging activities, most particularly in the large cities. A cadre told her that if they were prepared the enemy would not attack, but if they were unprepared the enemy most surely would attack.

The Nuclear Program

Between October 16, 1964, and June 26, 1973, China detonated fifteen nuclear devices, of which one was never acknowledged and is generally thought to have been a failure or an accident. Of the remaining fourteen, one was underground, one was delivered by a Soviet-type missile (of six hundred to one thousand mile range), and the rest were either tower shots or drops from TU-16s. Five tests were in the twenty kiloton range, five were in the twenty to five hundred kiloton range, and five were measured at one to three megatons. Analysts have speculated variously that the PRC was experimenting with tactical weapons for battlefield use, or aiming at early achievement of an MRBM capability, or perfecting a warhead for an ICBM. There are also cases to be made for IRBM development, and for perfection of a bomb for delivery by the TU-16. It is not impossible that all of these concepts have been entertained. Murphy reasons that the program "suggests continuing research aimed at the develop-

[25] *Strategic Survey 1971* (London: International Institute for Strategic Studies, 1972), p. 56.
[26] *Economic Assessment*, p. 106.

ment of a variety of compact weapons suitable for aircraft and missile delivery."[27] He notes that over a two-year period (1964-66), the yield-to-weight ratio of Chinese devices was improved tenfold. By 1970, the Chinese had developed a three-megaton warhead that could be delivered by an ICBM. High yield (one megaton) MRBM and IRBM warheads had not, at that time, been achieved. The construction of less powerful weapons in these classes is possible, and some authorities believe that this has been done.

Delivery vehicles for nuclear weapons include rockets and aircraft. It is generally agreed that naval forces do not yet have a nuclear capability, although a cruise missile of limited range for the "G" Class submarine is possible. So far as is known from open sources, there are not at present any ground artillery or troop-associated launchers capable of firing tactical nuclear weapons. The TU-16 aircraft is available in some numbers and has an action radius of 1,650 miles. In discussing China's nuclear weapons mix, Alice Hsieh[28] advances the admittedly controversial idea that the underground test of September 28, 1969, was a step in the development of a tactical weapon for fighter or fighter-bomber delivery.

The PRC has worked intensively on rocket vehicles. One nuclear test was made with a liquid-fuelled rocket with a range of less than a thousand kilometers. There was an extensive series of test firings in mid-1967, leading some observers to believe that proof testing and training programs were under way. If an initial operating capability had been achieved by that time, it is plausible that some eighty to a hundred MRBMs may now be deployed. Laird credited the PRC with the possible deployment of a "few" MR/IRBMs.[29] He also asserted that while the Chinese were focussing on liquid-fuelled missiles, there was some evidenc that they were also working on solid fuels. Moorer testified along the same lines, noting careful and deliberate movement toward longer-range missiles and fuel improvement. He also referred to the prospect of an ICBM by 1975, with earlier testing into the Pacific or Indian Oceans. A number of observers have called atten-

---

[27] *Murphy, loc. cit.*
[28] Alice Langley Hsieh, *Communist China's Evolving Military Strategy and Doctrine* (Washington: Institute for Defense Analyses, 1970), p. 49.
[29] *Laird*, p. 46.

tion to the presence of a fully instrumented ship that would be essential to such a test. There are also rumors of activity on the northern side of Mt. Everest and the west coast of Africa that might be associated with this program. Meanwhile, there have been reports that the PRC has conducted a test firing within its own territory (late 1970) of a reduced-range ICBM vehicle over a distance of 2,000-2,500 miles. Finally, the PRC has launched two space satellites, on April 24, 1970, and March 3, 1971. Although there is no precise agreement among analysts, there is a general consensus that these events demonstrate a growing ability to send heavier loads over greater distances, leading in turn to progress toward IRBM and ICBM capabilities.

The Chinese have consistently avoided discussion of their program except in political terms. A typical statement followed the twelfth test in November 1971:[30]

> . . . one of the necessary and limited nuclear tests conducted by China for the purpose of defense. The Chinese government declares once again that at no time and under no circumstances will China be the first to use nuclear weapons. The Chinese government and Chinese people will, as always, strive together with the other peoples and peaceloving countries in the world for the complete prohibition and thorough destruction of nuclear weapons.

Earlier, in July of that year, China had rejected the Soviet Union's proposal for a five-nation nuclear disarmament conference on the ground that *all* nations should participate. The PRC statement also repeated the usual Chinese claim that it was developing weapons only for defense and to break the imperialist monopoly.

In summary, it may be said that the Chinese nuclear program appears to embody the development of a useable range of warheads, mainly for aircraft and missile delivery. There is steady but prudent movement toward greater ranges. Authorities vary in their estimates of present holdings and program goals, but there is some consensus

---

[30] *Peking Review*, November 26, 1971.

about the near future. The PRC may have as few as ten or as many as a hundred MRBMs, with perhaps twenty deployed in the Northwest and Northeast, as well as "a small number" of IRBMs. Some ten to 25 ICBMs might on hand by 1975.

3

Some Conditioning Factors

The preceding chapter described the physical characteristics of the PLA and the directions in which the search for improved capabilities is moving. Before assessing the operational qualities of the forces, we have to examine certain other factors shaping their development and use.

Locations and Deployments

Military Balance gives probable location of divisions, other than artillery, as follows:[31]

---

[31] *Military Balance*, p. 44. The number of Military Regions has dropped from thirteen to eleven. The Tibet Region has been absorbed into Chengtu; and the Inner Mongolia Region divided among Shenyang, Peking, and Lanchou. A possible reason for this will be adduced later.

17

North and Northeast	40
(Shenyang and Peking MRs)	
East and Southeast	25
(Tsinan, Nanking, and Foochow MRs)	
South Central	20
(Canton and Wuhan MRs)	
Midwest	15
(Lanchou MR)	
West and Southwest	30
(Sinkiang, Chengtu, Kunming MRs)	

There are also fifteen to twenty thousand railway engineer and construction troops in North Vietnam and Laos, and the force aiding Hanoi may have been augmented recently. As far back as mid-1969, there was evidence of a strong Chinese response to Soviet deployments. An European observer noted half a million Chinese troops fairly close to the border, with strong concentrations in Inner Mongolia and Sinkiang. There were also said to be as many as four hundred fighter aircraft in Sinkiang.

These deployments indicate a sensible orientation of defenses. The large force in the North and Northeast is positioned to act quickly and in strength should the Soviet Union invade. It also has considerable capability to strike at the nearest, most vulnerable, and most important targets in Asian Russia: Khabarovsk, Vladivostok, and critical sections of the railway system. The units based on Tsinan may move north or east as the situation might demand. The other deployments seem to relate primarily to the defense of threatened areas, although they are also the proper places from which to mount attacks beyond the borders.

PLA naval forces are divided into three fleets—North, East, and South.[32] Together they cover the entire coast of China, with 240 vessels in the North, seven hundred in the East, and three hundred in the South. The presence of the Republic of China Navy in the Taiwan Strait inhibits free movement, and forces the PRC to transship to

[32] *Military Balance*, p. 45.

third country vessels at times. From time to time, there are clashes in the Strait in which some damage is done; but no large-scale battles have taken place, on sea or in the air, since the crisis of 1958. PLA naval forces do not seem to venture far from home. There have been reports of a "Chinese naval vessel" in the Indian Oecan, but its type, position, and course are shrouded in vagueness. The instrumented ship mentioned earlier has probably visited Sri Lanka.

Little is available in recent open literature on the location of air defense units, although a 1969 deployment indicates sensitivity to immediate threats. It appears that such units are distributed primarily to carry out basic air defense missions, with a substantial number of IL-28 light bombers oriented on Taiwan. The original eastward focus of the air defense radar net has been expanded to cover the South and North as well. Earlier crises produced appropriate deployments as in the Korean War and in 1962. Given the range and equipment of the PLA air force today, it is reasonable to assume that a further shift toward the northern borders has taken place.

Stratification of Roles

One of the determining factors of PLA effectiveness relates to the assigned roles and missions of particular units, and the state of their training and equipment. Nelsen makes clear that there is a primary separation between "regional" and "main force" units.[33] In tracing the PLA's activities during the Great Proletarian Cultural Revolution, he establishes that the former is made up of lightly armed, smaller units that owe some primary allegiance to a local (rather than central) authority. The responsiveness of these elements to Peking's directives will vary significantly with the nature of the tasks involved. "Main force" units, in contrast, are generally under central control, and great effort is made to keep them so. It is to these formations that newer and heavier weapons and equipment are assigned. They incorporate the interregional mobility and firepower that would be essential to a large-scale defense of the PRC, or to a

---

[33] Nelsen, *op. cit.*, pp. 8-14.

major movement beyond its borders. Some rotation of stations for these units has been reported.

Nelsen also states that the Public Security Bureaus almost disappeared as independent forces during the Cultural Revolution. Their function was absorbed into the PLA. This may help to account for reported increases of as much as half a million in PLA strength. Some temporary increase may also be accounted for by the extension of the obligatory service period, notably in the navy and air force. A recent increase of perhaps ten divisions has largely been a response to the tenseness of the situation along the border. During the Cultural Revolution, there was some evidence that the basic responsiveness of air and naval forces was to Peking, so that they also may be counted primarily as "main force" troops.

Training

The PLA publicizes very little about its state of training or general training programs. One of the political issues dividing Chinese military thinkers is the sharing out of the time of the regular forces as between training the militia and their own unit preparations. The continuing emphasis on the militia function suggests that the central leadership believes this component of "people's war" still has an important place in a widespread defense in depth, which is regarded as the primary mission of the PLA.

There does appear to be a steady and fairly high level of air defense training. This, plus the occasional flurry of praise for those credited with bringing down an intruder, testifies further to the concern over China's vulnerability under modern attack and to its overall preoccupation with defense.

Costs and Resource Allocation

The PLA is only one of the competitors for resources in a system burdened by chronic shortages. The speed of modernization and the acquisition of up-to-date material have been extensively debated within the military and between them and other bureaucratic interests. Without going into the principles underlying these differences, it is possible to learn something of the Chinese consensus from the visible results—keeping in mind that the PRC government has the ability, if it wills, to make drastic changes in plans and programs. Ashbrook states:[34]

> There is no direct information and little indirect evidence on the magnitude of China's military spending. To judge from the absolute size of its GNP, the size of its military establishment, and the percentage that defense takes of GNP in other major nations, however, defense almost certainly takes more than five percent of Chinese GNP and less than fifteen percent. In terms of manpower, the Chinese military establishment is roughly as large as those of the United States and the USSR. But the cost of maintaining the Chinese soldier is much lower. Moreover, the value of equipment and weapons purchased and operated is only a small fraction of that in the United States. On the other hand, China is involved in expensive missile and nuclear weapons development programs and appears to be rapidly expanding its military production. Although the problem of translating these programs into GNP values is difficult, ten percent seems to be a workable approximation of the share of defense in China's GNP.

Ashbrook gives the 1971 GNP of China as US $128 billion, or $150 per capita. Ten percent, $12.8 billion, looks small in comparison with defense expenditures in the United States or the Soviet Union; but it is not insignificant in itself and it demonstrates some earnestness and realism in the leadership. There are hard problems to be resolved in the future. Ashbrook calls attention to the "future burden on industry of serial manufacture and widespread deployment of missiles and other modern weapons." However the current level of defense spending was arrived at, and regardless of the com-

[34] Arthur G. Ashbrook "China: Economic Policy and Economic Results," in *Economic Assessment*, p. 45.

promises and adjustments that produced the present program and posture, it can be said that a level of defense effort tolerable to the leadership has been established and significant progress is being made within it. Whether the rate of force improvement is adequate for China's circumstances is another question, but each day that passes without actual combat is a bonus to Peking. The point at which China will determine that its forces are fully adequate for whatever it has in mind cannot be predicted; but rates of progress and program priorities will, as they unfold, provide further clues to what Peking conceives as an appropriate military posture.

In trying to assess the function of costs in the shaping of the PRC military policy, it is useful to remember that there is some flexibility. China is a *big* poor country, not a small poor country. An additional two dollars per capita per year over five years would produce over US $8 billion. This, reportedly, was just about the cost of the first five years of the French nuclear program, or about half the initial forecast cost of Japan's Fourth Defense Buildup Plan. It is not intended to suggest that Peking has any increase of that size in mind. But given the leadership's demonstrated ability to direct and control, China could, if concerned enough over its safety, or intent on major aggression, expand its present effort substantially.

An interesting event—the "steel *versus* electronics" issue—has recently furnished some material for speculating on Chinese Communist defense thinking. Edwin F. Jones sees this question as a difference in view over the relative importance of basic economic needs and exotic military requirements.[35] Others have also referred to this controversy as an internal struggle over the allocation of resources to military programs, particularly to nuclear weapons, and there is some primary evidence for this. A letter emanating from a group within the Ministry of Metallurgical Industry recalls Mao's injunction to develop industry with "steel as the key link;" the mistaken notion that electronics be "taken as the center" is attributed to that all-purpose villain, Liu Shao-ch'i. An involved argument supports heavy industry and associated extractive and service functions as the

---

[35] Edwin F. Jones, "The Cultural Revolution: In Search of a Maoist Model," in *ibid.*, p. 57.

key to progress, and repeats the classic Maoist point that "compared with economy, politics cannot but take the first position." Electronics is dismissed as a processing industry.

This letter has been interpreted as a policy statement repudiating those who would seek an accelerated and more sophisticated nuclear program at too great a resource cost. Since impressive progress is visible in both the steel and electronics industries, it may be that there are concealed signals and purposes in the letter. It could very well relate to a dispute over the general thrust of military development; equally, it could be the expression of a difference between central and regional authorities or between strategic and regional forces. But however interpreted, there is still a convincing body of evidence that Chinese industry is now performing well in support of military modernization.

Production Facilities

The general policy for locating production facilities in China is summarized by Field in these terms:[36]

> In 1952, when about three quarters of total industrial production and more than eighty percent of the ferrous metallurgy and machine building industries were located in the coastal area, the Chinese considered themselves peculiarly vulnerable to foreign attack. This concentration of modern industry in the coastal provinces was a major consideration in the decision to locate in China's interior 472 out of the 694 major industrial projects listed in the First Five Year Plan."

This program had only indifferent success. The number of major production centers upon which the building of military equipment depends has expanded only slightly, even though a very large number of small factories have appeared in the interior and in rural areas. These plants relate more to consumer goods production and agricul-

---

[36] Robert Michael Field, "Chinese Industrial Development: 1949-1970," in *ibid.*, p. 70.

tural needs. The electronics industry may be an exception. Reichers says[37] that there are about two hundred major plants, employing four hundred thousand persons, and five hundred smaller ones. There are six major centers and another six in which significant production facilities exist. Some of these plants are located in the interior, as are those in other categories of production, but this fact may be losing some of its military relevance. Duplication and hardening are much more important in an age of nuclear weapons, or even in a conventional situation where an attacker might be expected to gain some control of the air.

There are some other critical situations in the Chinese production system. There are probably no more than three plants producing material for nuclear weapons, including a new hardened facility somewhere in the interior. There are three major airframe producers, and probably only one making jet engines. The number of sites producing tanks and artillery is small. Production facilities for smaller weapons and trucks seem to be more widely distributed over the countryside.

What emerges from this admittedly cursory survey is a picture of great vulnerability, particularly but not exclusively to nuclear attack. If the mainland were actually under attack, it would be difficult to maintain any useful level of production or to move major items from the points of production to units in the field.

Technology and Quality

It is often pointed out that the PRC lags behind the Soviet Union, the United States, and Japan in technology and sophistication of products. This is generally true, but on occasion the Chinese have demonstrated a skill that surprised the rest of the world. The important question is usefulness. "The best is the enemy of good." This is nowhere more true than in military hardware. In every case, it is necessary to assess the meaning of comparative quality. In some cases

---

[37] Reichers, *op. cit.*, pp. 91-92.

—aircraft, ASW *versus* submarines—a technical superiority can be decisive. In others, the apparent superiority of one side over another may lie in "gold-plating" or in levels of sophistication that have very slight payoffs in battle.

4

Capabilities and Limitations of the PLA

The physical attributes of the PLA define a range of military tasks it can perform. This chapter addresses the problem of measuring PLA abilities in relation to the actual military operations that Peking might be forced to, or elect to, conduct. Three general cases are postulated: defense of the homeland; excursions beyond China's borders over continuous lines of communication; and excursions over discontinuous lines. The role of nuclear weapons will be considered in each case. In addition, the military role of forces in being in the conduct of foreign relations, and their contribution to foreign aid (direct and covert), will also be dealt with.

The types and levels of enemy forces involved will necessarily be a major Chinese consideration in any specific encounter. Here it is proposed simply to generalize about these factors and not to examine them in detailed scenarios. Neither is it intended to take a "worst case" approach, endowing the PLA with capabilities based simply on weapons inventories.

26

Defense of the Homeland

Any attempt at a general conquest and occupation of China faces the classic problems of space and density. An invader would do well to select a relatively small number of major targets for destruction or capture, and from that position attempt to negotiate an acceptable outcome. This immediately raises the question of how much of China must be seized and held (or destroyed) in order to bring Peking to negotiations. There is also the possibility that an invader might establish independent political units under local officials. Except in minority regions—most particularly Sinkiang—the latter alternative seems less likely.

In the first case, while it might be possible fairly quickly to reduce substantially the industrial base and military resupply systems, there would be no way to know how much essential war material was dispersed and concealed. Thus it would be difficult to gauge the endurance of China's conventional forces, or the time and rate at which the balance of struggle would shade into guerrilla activity. Meanwhile, the shortening of lines of communication would reduce the supply problem for PRC forces in the field (subject to the possible loss of resupply sources for some major items).

The conduct of an irregular "people's war" and of conventional war simultaneously would pose some problems in communications, command, and control for the PLA. These have long been recognized. In 1938, Mao said:[38]

> Coordination with the regular forces in battles, in actual fighting on the battlefield, is the task of all guerrilla units in the vicinity of an interior-line battlefield . . . a guerrilla (unit) has to perform whatever task it is assigned by the commander of the regular forces, which is usually to pin down some of the enemy's forces, disrupt his supply lines, conduct reconnaissance, or act as guides for the regular forces.

---

[38] Mao Tse-tung, "Problems of Strategy in Guerrilla War Against Japan," in *Selected Works,* second edition (Peking: Foreign Languages Press, 1966), vol. 2, p. 92.

Mao's work demonstrates that the concerted action of several types of forces has been clearly thought out. It can be assumed that strategic and regional forces would act together effectively, and make full use of all types of militia, despite any differences they may have had in the past or the technical problems of coordination. The military advantages of the "sea of people" are uniquely the property of the homeland defender—a fact noted by many military thinkers before Mao, including Clausewitz. The actual distribution of tasks among the several elements would be dictated by circumstances, but an invader could be sure that he would face them all. If invaded, China could muster as many as ten million fighters of all types. The invader's security problems at rest or on the move would be formidable. As he penetrated the interior, he would have to engage PLA forces through successive positions of some depth.

Given the location of industrial and military production facilities, the Chinese probably would not opt for a uniform defense of all land areas, based on interior lines. Some variation of perimeter-type defenses, allowing some enemy penetration (which could be described as "luring in deep") would be more realistic. This would, of course, give the invader some freedom in, or even control, of the interstices—subject, however, to the actions of local irregulars and a hostile population. Under these conditions, the attacker's supply and communication lines would become more vulnerable, particularly if several strategic areas were under simultaneous assault. Equally, Chinese forces would retain some ability to reinforce and cooperate laterally.

Naval forces would have some part in this sort of defense, particularly if a substantial part of the invading force came by sea. This condition would maximize the effective use of the submarine fleet and the large number of defense and patrol-type units. Even so, considering that only the United States or the Soviet Union could mount such an attack, the long-term endurance of PLA naval forces would be doubtful.

All of the above considerations are based on the overriding assumption that the PLA would be able to avoid yielding mastery of the air. Plane for plane, the invaders would probably be superior.

Offsetting this would be the factor of sheer numbers, an improving surface-to-air capability, and optimum operating conditions—shorter distances, home fields, stable warning systems. Over time, the feeder system for spares and fuel would weaken under attack, and the Chinese air forces would be bound to lose much of their effectiveness. The problem for the invader would be the size of the effort needed to achieve this condition in several locations, to maintain it, and finally to ensure that his own air forces were properly used. Widespread guerrilla activity is not economically amenable to suppression from the air.

Should the Soviet Union be the attacker, the PLA would have a number of possibilities for counteraction. It would be very difficult to prevent the Chinese from cutting off the rail line between Khabarovsk and Vladivostok. Supplying the area thus isolated by sea would be a difficult task. The extensive resources of the area would undergo early attrition, and the naval forces stationed there would suffer. The rail line is equally vulnerable at many other points, and its destruction would reduce substantially the long-term logistical endurance of all Soviet territory east of any break. The unanswerable question here is the level of supply support for Soviet garrisons that might be on hand when fighting started. There is some reason to believe that the day-to-day maintenance of the reported one million Soviet troops along the border already poses a sizeable problem, and leaves only thin margins for stockpiling against what could be a long and exhausting campaign.

The introduction of nuclear weapons in a "defense of the homeland" situation would revise all previous estimates. If use were restricted to tactical (battlefield) weapons, the PRC could expect to suffer major damage to all units and installations that stood in the path of an invasion. Should larger, longer-range weapons be introduced, China would experience the loss of the major part of the industrial base and infrastructure won at such high cost and effort over the past 23 years. The level of damage—and what was left to support recovery—would be determined solely by the attacker. If, as time goes on, the Chinese attain significant despersion and hardening of production facilities, there could be some limitation of first-strike destruction. Even so, and even if the major nuclear production facilities were relocated to some safer place, such as Tibet, China could expect to lose whatever part of its weapons production system the enemy considered it necessary to destroy.

What could the PRC do with its nuclear weapons in a "defense of the homeland" situation? The weapons program described earlier hints at interest in a varied family of weapons. The numbers predicted to be operationally available in the several categories as of mid-1972 have variously been estimated to be: MRBMs, ten to a hundred; IRBMs, "a few" to thirty; ICBMs, a number of observed acts may be related to the testing of a long-range weapon, but (despite recurring predictions) no warhead or vehicle has yet been fired over the full ICBM distance. This event would start the clock on an initial operational capability of ten to 25 weapons perhaps five years further on in time. Thus endowed, the PRC would at best be capable of supporting a deterrent strategy of meaningful proportions. With medium-range weapons, all of Japan may be placed under fire. That nation is uniquely vulnerable—a fact that has not escaped the notice of Japanese politicians and military men. It is not only entirely within range of land-based medium-range weapons; in addition, no point in Japan is more than 75 miles from the sea. The destruction of ten major target areas in Honshu would account for more than sixty percent of Japan's industrial capacity.

With Japan as hostage, the PRC might have an effective deterrent against United States first use. This raises the question of whether the Soviet Union now has a similar linkage with India. If, as has been reported, the PRC has accelerated its IRBM program, the value of India as a hostage for Moscow's good behavior decreases, since a reasonable IRBM array poses a direct threat to important targets in metropolitan Russia itself. A similar capability against the United States has to await the attainment of some significant ICBM force. Alice Hsieh, after analysis of the overall situation in which China finds itself, concludes that the following are the objectives of its entire nuclear weapons effort:[39]

---

[39] Hsieh, *op. cit.*, pp. 60-61.

(1) the enhancement of China's international political stature;

(2) in the event of an evolving crisis situation, the deterrence of a United States attack on the China mainland as well as the imposition of restraints on United States military policies in the area;

(3) the undermining of the United States-Asian alliance and security arrangements;

(4) the inhibition of Asian nations' self-defense efforts;

(5) the fostering of internal instability in underdeveloped areas and, where the chances of success appear high, national liberation movements; and

(6) the enhancement of the role of China's conventional forces.

Hsieh's analysis focuses heavily on the political factor that is always so prominent in Peking's thinking. It is pertinent to add one mild caution in the light of recent events. Soviet support for India and Bangladesh, together with the recent substantial additions to Soviet forces along the border with China, may have increased Peking's interest in weapons purely as weapons, although it is still not possible to support in logic any Chinese first strike strategy.

On balance, it may be said that the PRC has impressive capabilities for the defense of the homeland. Despite Russian criticism of what they describe as primitive concepts of modern war, the Chinese have concentrated on maximizing their capabilities within a rational concept of the requirements of a defensive war. If Peking's nuclear deterrent operates (or if an invader refrains from the use of these weapons for any of a number of reasons), the operational climate would favor the defender for a number of reasons:

Transportation and communications problems would have less effect on the defense of critical areas on interior lines than would be the case in excursions beyond China's borders.

The presence of an alien invader would override any previous internal rivalries.[40]

Strategic forces, regional forces, and several types of militia would combine into forces of formidable size and a great range of capabilities.

The "mix" of forces—conventional and irregular—would be most effective in interior defense. The invader would be subjected to a wide range of actions, and the periods between major battles would be characterized by guerrilla attacks and general civilian hostility.

If the attacker were the Soviet Union, the PRC would have a great opportunity to counterattack over the Ussuri River, cutting the railroad and isolating Vladivostok, a major element in the total Soviet strategic system in the Far East.

Large-scale defense of the homeland is not without problems and handicaps:

The fractionated force structure and the attendant complexity of the command and control machinery have great latent possibilities for confusion and wasted effort.

The high concentration of industrial activity and production facilities creates vulnerable targets for bombing, even with conventional weapons. Problems of distance and logistics for air defense would be minimized, but the tasks involved in protecting vital places would be of such size as to set an exhausting rate of operations.

The location of military equipment production facilities is such that extensive damage to, or isolation of, a small number of key plants—such as aircraft and tank factories—would cut

---

[40] Chalmers Johnson, in *Peasant Nationalism and Communist Power* (Stanford: Stanford University Press, 1962), gives convincing demonstrations of the motivational effects of such a presence in case studies of China and Yugoslavia.

sharply into the combat endurance of the PLA nationwide, in spite of the relocation mentioned earlier.

The truck and rail transportation network, although much improved over the past twenty years, is still subject to interdiction. Extensive damage would seriously reduce the PLA's ability to reinforce and to coordinate laterally or to maintain major supply systems.

Excursions Beyond Borders—Continuous LOCs

Should the PRC elect to send forces into adjacent territory, whether for aggression, counterattack, or preemption, there would begin almost immediately some degradation of combat effectiveness. Logistics problems, which were serious enough in the Korean setting, would be magnified by the demands of more modern weapons and the vehicles of the improved forces. The important support of friendly militia and civilians would disappear at the border and, in some cases, be replaced by active hostility. The Chinese would also face a difficult decision over the number of troops they might want to deploy abroad in any particular venture. If, as many think, the regional forces are not immediately and completely at the disposal of the central command, some difficult choices and balancing acts would be required.

There is also the nagging possibility that a foe on one flank might see an opportunity to act while China was occupied elsewhere, although this situation could arise any time PRC forces were engaged at home or abroad. The PRC might not enjoy the security of a sanctuary and interference with lines of communication would reach back into the homeland, inevitably influencing the ability to maintain sizeable forces beyond its borders for an extended time. Having said this, there is still the lesson of Korea. Part of the Chinese LOC came under heavy attack, but they were still able to support almost a million men under increasingly difficult conditions.

Given the conditions of today, it is reasonable to say that oper-

FERNALD LIBRARY
COLBY-SAWYER
NEW LONDON

ations over the border by large PLA forces are quite possible, but their cost would be a critical factor in determining their feasibility. The examples of the advantages of speed of execution and the ability to select targets, as exemplified in the Arab-Israeli conflict in 1967 and the more recent Indian triumph in Bangladesh, have not been lost on Asian nations. The political ambience would have great influence on Chinese actions, but the ability to confront the world with a *fait accompli* would be a potential asset in any Chinese attack on a neighboring country. Tibet stands as an example of what the PRC can and will do when it senses that there is no outside protector of the target country.

While ground force improvements in the PLA include greater fire-power, increased tactical and logistical mobility, and improved communications, there is little open evidence that much attention has been given to the problems of air operations from expeditionary airfields, or concentration of highly mobile air defense ground weapons for related use. The numbers and types of helicopters on hand and the construction rate at present do not imply any strong priority for troop-carrying helicopters of the types used in vertical envelopment tactics. Naval forces do not appear to be making extensive preparations to operate along coastal areas in support of a major land campaign. With the capabilities they do have, the PLA could mount and sustain operations large enough to impose its will on any of its smaller neighbors, provided the United States or the Soviet Union had not previously established the level and mix of aid and commitment necessary to withstand the Chinese effort. It would be dangerous for Peking to assume that the big powers would withhold the needed support.

It must be concluded that the risks and costs of ground action beyond Chinese borders would be acceptable to Peking only if the PRC saw military action as absolutely necessary to protect its own position, or as not likely to involve a third party as a supporter of the invaded country. In addition, China might feel obligated to pay the price of intervention if the complete destruction of an Asian Communist leadership appeared to be the probable outcome of a deteriorating situation. With the possible exception of action in behalf of Hanoi of Pyongyang, the PRC would be looking over its shoulder at the Soviet Union if it should become heavily engaged elsewhere. In short, the PRC has the military resources to initiate action against other nations in Asia; but in some cases, the unforeseeable reactions of Moscow and Washington would require a very large and open-ended commitment that would not seem to be worthwhile unless there were a clear and immediate threat to China's security, or the total defeat of a major ally were imminent.

Although, as Hsieh has pointed out,[41] the PRC may be experimenting with the development of tactical nuclear weapons, there is as yet no clear evidence that battlefield types are being produced. The role of nuclear weapons in foreign excursions would largely be the deterrence of antagonists, working to ensure a nuclear-free battlefield.

Excursions Beyond Borders—Discontinuous LOCs

When the PRC comes to consider operations over water or from the air, it faces immediately the problem of adequate transport. It simply does not exist. The amphibious portion of the navy is hopelessly inadequate and obsolete. There is no indication of a significant building program. To attempt an invasion of, say, Taiwan would at present require the assembly and movement of a motley fleet of small commercial ships, junks, and the few available merchant ships (all in the ten thousand ton range). To make the passage, it would be necessary first to establish air superiority and then to gain control of the sea. The first would be terribly costly; and, unless it were achieved, the second would also be well-nigh impossible. Under such conditions, it is difficult to imagine a PRC force crossing the hundred-mile Taiwan Strait and landing against resistance. The cost of such a venture would be completely prohibitive if the United States Seventh Fleet became involved under the terms of the treaty with the Republic of China on Taiwan.

---

[41] Alice Langley Hsieh, "China's Nuclear Missile Programme: Regional or Intercontinental?" *China Quarterly* (January-March 1971), p. 98.

Airborne attack—for example, against Asians—offers equally grim prospects. Even by drafting the new additions to the civil air fleet, the PLA could not land and support anything larger than a light division for any period of time without opening a supplementary line of communication overland. The air defense of any prospective target would effectively forestall such an effort.

Nuclear weapons would not add to PRC capabilities in such operations in any positive sense. They would invite swift and heavy retaliation. Further, there are real inhibitions against using these weapons against other Asians, most particularly the people of Taiwan. Here again, the Chinese nuclear capability is principally useful to deter others; and, under circumstances that might indicate early United States resort to nuclear weapons, perhaps to intimidate Japan into refusing base accommodations to the United States. The actual use of nuclear weapons would probably provoke retaliation from the United States or Soviet Union, with disastrous results for the mainland.

Subsidiary Roles for the PLA

A function of armed forces that does not relate to actual fighting is the political role of forces in being. The simple existence of capable armed forces can influence the conduct of foreign affairs and the nature of international relations. Some such quality does accrue to the PLA, but it is inhibited by the power of the deterrents mentioned above. Nevertheless, the ability of the PRC to influence or intimidate other Asian nations will relate in some degree to its credible military power. This power will be viewed by its potential targets in terms of the *total* military balance—that is, the degree to which the United States or the Soviet Union will act to offset it.

In gauging the strength and utility of the PLA, there is still another dimension in its contribution to Peking's programs of military assistance to Third World clients—both to governments and to subversive groups in selected areas. These programs include the use of PLA personnel as workers, instructors, and advisors, as well as supplies of military weapons and equipment. This activity can best be assessed by some actual examples.

In Southeast Asia, Chinese support takes a variety of forms. Arms and other support flow to leftist groups in Burma, Cambodia, and Laos. While it is hard to measure the dollar value of such help, it helps to keep its recipients in business and maintains the PRC claim to a major role in the affairs of the area. It has been asserted that almost a million AK-47 rifles have been supplied to Viet Cong forces in South Vietnam. Military aid to the North, although much less than that furnished by the Soviet Union, has nevertheless amounted to US $750 million, with the bulk of this amount arriving since 1966. There have been perhaps as many as forty thousand PLA troops in North Vietnam at various times. While they have not been directly engaged in combat with United States or Saigon forces, they provide the essential skills for the maintenance of railroads, antiaircraft protection for railway repair units, and some forms of logistical support.

There is inescapable military significance in the Chinese road building program along its borders. The road connecting Tibet and Sinkiang through the Aksai Chin area is a major issue between India and the PRC. The PRC has built roads in Pakistan, connecting Gilgit with points in Tibet and Sinkiang; between Yunnan and Dienbienphu through Northern Laos; and in Nepal. Most of this work has been done or supervised by PLA engineers.

Farther afield, the PLA has been the principal military supporter of Pakistan in recent years, providing such items as Mig and IL-28 aircraft, tanks, and other equipment. Peking has recently undertaken a new US $300 million aid program to Pakistan, which includes one-for-one replacement of the losses of the Bangladesh War. Various subversive elements such as the Naxalite movement in West Bengal have also gotten some military support.

The PRC has given help to some Middle Eastern clients in the Arabian Peninsula (South Yemen, Dhofar) and to several Palestinian groups. This has included miltary training on site and in China, and the provision of small arms, mortars, rocket launchers, and ammunition. Modest aid to Egypt is overshadowed by the massive Soviet program, but the PRC does manage to keep the channels open, reinforcing small-scale physical assistance with vociferous political support.

Much has been made of China's most ambitious aid program— the Tan-Zam railroad. Less noticed has been a sizeable military assistance effort in Tanzania that has provided some US $40 million worth of aircraft, tanks, and naval patrol craft. Peking now has a "piece of the action" in any black-white confrontation in that area. Albania has been heavily supplied with military equipment since 1960. There has been much evidence of Chinese military support to other clients, including Indonesia (before 1965), North Korea, and the Sihanouk government in Cambodia before it was overthrown. Chinese weapons are appearing in some numbers with the insurgent forces in the Philippines. And there are no doubt others.

The most meaningful function of the PLA may be its role in PRC foreign aid policy, which in turn is based on carefully chosen political considerations. The material drawn from PLA stocks, while not inconsiderable, does not constitute a major drain on resources. In many cases, it would appear that older items are supplied when their performance is adequate for the client's requirements. The manpower involved at any one time cannot be seen as affecting the basic combat capabilities of the Chinese armed forces.

5

Threats to Security—The View From Peking

The development of military policy in the PRC has gone through much debate and change in the political process. Whatever the issues may have been, there is now at least partially visible a conceptual framework of perceived military threats to national security and foreign policy goals set by the national leadership. Chinese security perceptions can be defined and ordered, and the "fit" (or lack of it) between missions thus developed and force structures can be subjected to analysis. To be sure, competing solutions to the same problem are bound to evolve, and differing interpretations of the threat produce conflicting views over appropriate responses. Hence, any attempt to reconstruct a Chinese "Estimate of the Situation" is bound to be tentative, and changes in Peking's assessment of enemies and dangers are bound to occur. In discussing PRC "security" concepts, the use of military forces for asserting hegemony or for preemptive action are of course included. The development of a capability to defend effectively against any sort of major threat implies, within some limits, the prospective ability to use the forces in tasks other than defense.

What Does China See?

It is sometimes argued that the PRC sees itself as beleaguered, and that much of its military action since 1949 has been response to a perceived threat to its security or territorial integrity. Further, it is sometimes said that China's quarrels with some of its neighbors turn on unresolved territorial and border problems, rather more than on larger questions of overall relations. For the time being, these considerations can be put aside in the interest of concentrating on the search for symmetry between military tasks shaped by strategic concerns and force postures and improvement programs.

The Soviet Union. As Michael Tatu has asserted,[42] Sino-Russian enmity has a much longer, more intense, and more continuous history than does Sino-American rivalry. For immediate purposes, however, only fairly recent events need be examined. Moscow's unwillingness to act with appropriate aggressiveness in a number of events, particularly from the time of the 1958 Taiwan Strait crisis onward, deeply offended the Chinese. Peking felt a major shock when Soviet forces intervened in Czechoslovakia in 1968. This was intensified when an ideological justification for this intervention was enunciated in the socalled Brezhnev Doctrine. If the Soviet Union had a basic and natural right to intervene in the internal political affairs of another Socialist state, then China's vulnerability as a dissident and competing force became all too apparent.

Without attempting to fix the sequence of initiatives, Soviet forces did, during a series of publicized armed clashes in 1969, find several occasions to chastise local PLA units in well-planned and executed small encounters. As relations grew more tense, the Soviet Union played on China's fears. There was a rumor that Soviet diplomats were sounding other nations as to how they might react to a pre-

---

[42] *London Times*, January 5, 1971.

emptive nuclear strike against the PRC. Some of the Warsaw Pact countries hinted that they might send forces to Asia to support Russia. Although the attempt was frustrated, the Soviet Union did make strong efforts to censure the Chinese in international Communist Party councils. Moscow also lectured Peking about the latter's military backwardness. Scarcely two weeks after the first Ussuri River incident, Soviet broadcasts warned the people of China that rockets, against which there was no defense, formed the backbone of the Soviet armed forces, and that the Soviets possessed the most up-to-date aircraft. China, they said, had nothing to match this, and, indeed, had no other modern offensive weaponry. Moscow Radio also pointed to "some countries" as backward and unscientific in military theory, and ridiculed the idea of protracted war as outdated in the nuclear age. "This oversimplified theory of the defensive, which was nursed in those remote days of guerrilla warfare," is now "being applied to modern warfare."

The Soviets have not been satisfied with mere polemics. *Strategic Survey 1971* presents a picture of increasing physical pressure along the border, with the number of regular divisions in the border area and Outer Mongolia rising from thirty in 1970 to 44 in 1971. The latest models of aircraft and surface-to-surface missiles were reported to be present in substantial numbers. Some tactical boundaries were redrawn, and the Soviet commanders assigned to the area had excellent qualifications and reputations. Altogether, the Soviet posture could not be seen as seriously preparing for the conduct of war.

Washington Post columnists[43] have asserted that the PRC has abandoned its earlier defense posture of maintaining only light screening forces forward, and has begun to move heavy, first-line units closer to the line of contact. William Beecher reinforces this analysis: "China seems to be abandoning her old defensive concept of deploying primarily poorly equipped militia and paramilitary units along the border to draw Soviet divisions deep into Chinese territory before attempting to engage them with regular troops to the front and guer-

---

[43] Joseph Alsop, June 23, 1972; and Jack Anderson, June 29, 1972.

rilla units to the rear. Instead . . . she has recently been moving several first-line army divisions and air force squadrons to forward positions."[44] These Chinese moves are clearly in response to an upgrading of Soviet capabilities and perceived intentions. In addition, the PRC has moved to invest the necessary resources to react more directly to the new situation. Beecher states that the PRC is believed to have deployed fifteen to thirty 600-mile missiles and five to fifteen 1,500-mile IRBMs for this purpose. A tantalizing question, at this time unanswerable, is whether Chinese behavior is due entirely to a changed estimate of the threat, or whether its shifting posture represents a new plateau of ability to field more and better weapons. From a somewhat different perspective, Joseph C. Harsh says he was informed that the PRC had mounted a battery of short-range missiles aimed at Vladivostok.[45] "In other words," he says, "the Russians have missed the boat. Had they wanted to prevent China from becoming a full-scale nuclear power, they should have acted before China came into possession of its own deterrent. Even one nuclear missile targeted on Vladivostok is quite a deterrent. The Chinese, it seems, have more than one, and can hit more than one Russian target." Jack Anderson cites "intelligence reports" to the same effect in a later column.[46] All this suggests that Peking's conceptual optimal mix of forces is not so rigidly bound by doctrine to militia and second-line units as it is conditioned by the availability of more sophisticated weaponry.

It is apparent that Peking has positioned a very large proportion of its forces in reaction to Soviet stimuli. The forty divisions (up seven over the previous year) reported in the North and Northeast, the fifteen (up four over the previous year) in Lanchou Military Region, and a share of those assigned to the South Central area (Tsinan) and to the West and Southwest area (Sinkiang) account for more than half the total number of strategic force divisions. Looking at physical posture and preparations, including the extensive digging of shelters, and putting aside the themes and variations of propaganda and polemics, it would appear that the PRC now

---

[44] Beecher, *op. cit.*
[45] *Christian Science Monitor*, August 15, 1972.
[46] *Washington Post*, August 27, 1972.

sees the Soviet Union as the prime threat to its physical security, and is devoting the major share of its military resources and effort to dealing with that threat. The general strategic stance is defensive, although it must be kept in mind that a strategic defense also involves the ability to attack in force, either to preempt or to retaliate. It is entirely possible that neither side wants war. But a dangerous game of increasing forces and reducing cushioning space between the sides is now being played, and misunderstanding is always possible.

The United States. The PRC's catalog of differences with the United States includes a number of cases in which military factors are prominent. For illustrative purposes, four particular situations have special significance: American support for the Republic of China on Taiwan; the United States role in Southeast Asia; the Japan-US Security Treaty; and United States support for the Republic of Korea. All of these have served to justify a substantial United States military presence in areas uncomfortably close to mainland China, and to involve commitments that nullify any aspirations for Chinese hegemony through military force.

Peking's long-term hostility over these issues has survived pretty much intact through the period of changing Sino-American relations, even though public statements and political actions may vary with the changing scenario. The United States is still denounced over the war in Indochina and for its support of South Korea. Vows to "liberate" Taiwan are repeated regularly, and maneuvers to weaken the Japanese relationship persist. The United States is still the exemplar of capitalist and imperialist military adventurism, even if its place as an enemy of China must be shared with the Soviet Union.

To be sure, the physical scene is somewhat different, and China must feel some reduction in the sense of direct military threat from the United States. Peking has had several assurances, going back at least as far as 1962, that the United States will not attack the mainland or support such an operation. The US Navy's Taiwan Strait Patrol has been stopped; and in any case, except for the operational rotation of small air units, there has never been a significant United States attack force based there. As far back as 1969-70, Congressional testimony elicited that United States forces on the island of Taiwan included: (a) the United States Taiwan Defense Command Headquarters, a planning staff with no forces assigned, and only 192 military personnel; (b) Air Force support for Vietnam, a force of some nine thousand that is now phasing down as its missions in connection with air logistical support decrease; and (c) the Military Assistance Advisory Group, with something slightly under five hundred personnel performing the duties normally associated with such units.[47] There are, in addition, small intelligence and communications detachments. The White House has refused a request to transfer to Taiwan any nuclear weapons that might be displaced from Okinawa as a result of reversion to Japan. All this can be taken to show that the United States, while firm in its commitment to protect the ROC, is not developing Taiwan as a base for attack on the PRC, nor will it support such a venture by others. Although by no means satisfying Peking's demands, this does mitigate its concern over military action from Taiwan.

The withdrawal of American ground forces from Indochina reduces the possibility that the United States might contemplate a ground attack against South China. The maintenance and extensive use of air and naval forces in the area must, however, create some concern in Peking. Chinese planners no doubt study and evaluate the effects of United States air and naval attacks in Indochina. This can only accentuate an awareness of Chinese vulnerabilities and the problems of defense should either the Soviet Union or the United States elect to attack in this fashion. Despite considerable celebration when a stray United States aircraft or reconaissance drone is brought down, there is no evidence of confidence in their ability to cope with large-scale attacks. For the time being, China will have to rely on political deterrence rather than military power in dealing with the physical challenge of the United States. Current trends in Sino-American relations suggest that there is little likelihood of an American attack, but the military threat exists.

---

[47] *United States Security Agreements and Commitments Abroad, Republic of China, Hearings before the Subcommittee on United States Security Agreements and Commitments Abroad, Committee on Foreign Relations, United States Senate, Part 4, 1969-1970,* p. 1004.

The combination of American and Japanese resources in a war against the PRC would be a formidable menace to Chinese security. The Security Treaty and associated arrangements are, therefore, seen as the embodiment of a real physical threat. In Peking's thinking, the loss of active Japanese support, most particularly the use of Japanese bases, would reduce the US ability to attack the mainland or assist Taiwan. Japan is seen as a tool or associate enhancing the military power of the United States. The PRC must, on balance, welcome Japanese assumption of control over Okinawa, and be encouraged by the trend in the internal Japanese defense debate, which seems to be running in favor of some dilution of defense ties with the United States.

United States support for the Republic of Korea translates, in PRC thinking, into another focus of United States military power in an area directly threatening China. It also requires Peking to maintain a fairly high level of support for the North. United States troop reductions in South Korea, while of course wlecome to Peking, do not wholly relieve this concern. So long as the ROK is willing to permit United States bases on its territory, the Chinese must be concerned over the presence or reentry of United States air and naval forces, or the forward stationing of ground troops that can be used against the mainland. The South Korean force envisioned in the Nixon Doctrine would not in itself threaten mainland China.

In the larger view, Peking still sees a formidable United States military presence along its eastern and southern borders. While ground forces have been reduced, the demonstrated ability to maintain very high rates of air and naval operations is far from reassuring. The physical menace exists in a form against which the PLA is probably least able to defend. The best defense here lies in political action to reduce the chances that the United States would strike. The raw military facts constitute a major threat.

Japan. China's view of Japan as a military power in East Asia has deep historical roots. This can account for some of Peking's expressed concern over the alleged resurgence of Japanese militarism. Of perhaps more immediate importance is the possibility that Japan could assume a role in the protection of South Korea or Taiwan, or substitute for the United States in the prosecution of Asian conflicts—in effect, "using Asians to fight imperialism's wars in Asia."

Chou En-lai has emphasized Chinese Communist concern over Japanese militarism on several occasions, but with interesting qualifications at times. In his interview with James Reston, Chou mentioned the inevitable linkage between economic and military expansion, the size of Japan's Fourth Defense Buildup Plan (at that time, before revaluation of the yen, about US $16 billion), and the attitudes of the Japanese people as implied by a recent film and by the Mishima suicide.[48] On other occasions, Chou has seemed to concede that Chinese concern over Japanese militarism was directed less to any immediate threat than to the potential of Japanese ambition and abilities. He told a Yugoslav journalist that "the revival of Japanese militarism and the modernization of Japanese troops also require time."[49] The general content of Chinese statements on this subject suggests that Japan is being warned that it is under surveillance by all who remember World War II, and that its growing economic power must not be translated into military expansion.

The Japanese defense program makes clear that Japan has no immediate intention of building significant offensive power. The trend of opinion in Japan suggests a modest (and largely ineffective) tendency toward militarism; but this is not yet a serious problem. There is a running political quarrel in Tokyo over the cost and content of the Fourth Defense Buildup Plan. Chinese pressures have reinforced those who would reduce armament costs and any appearance of offensive capability. The immediate result has been the deletion of a number of aircraft and fleet unit types from a defense-oriented program that, to start with, had only the most modest convertibility to offensive capabilities. In brief, while Japan certainly has the economic and industrial means for developing large offensive forces, conventional and nuclear, over the next several years, Tokyo seems to have no interest or desire to move in these directions. At present, Japan

[48] *New York Times*, August 10, 1971.
[49] Dara Jankeovic, in *Vjesnik* (Zagreb), August 28, 1971; reprinted in FBIS, August 31, 1971.

has no capability to move against the mainland. Peking understands this, and devotes its political energies to heading off future Japanese military adventurism. But as an ally of the United States, Japan must be dealt with by some level of military response. It is here, perhaps, that a "hostage" nuclear strategy can have its greatest payoff.

India and Others. India and the PRC have longstanding differences over borders, in addition to the political rivalries that inhere in their differing political and economic positions. The end of the Sino-Indian conflict of 1962 saw the Chinese in a strong position to maintain their hold over disputed border areas. The geographical position has changed little since then, but the military balance between the two nations has altered considerably. The Bangladesh War demonstrated new levels of effectiveness in the Indian forces, and—perhaps of even greater import—a strong Soviet commitment to political and material support for New Delhi. China saw its client Pakistan take a humiliating beating, and did not react effectively. How much China was constrained by the August 1971 Soviet-Indian Treaty, and how much by objective physical conditions, is a matter for speculation. The Indians did maintain a strong garrison along the border. There have been reports that Moscow threatened action in Sinkiang if China interfered in the subcontinent; and it was Soviet fleet units that reacted to the United States task force in the Bay of Bengal. The missile boats of the Indian Navy that sank a Pakistani destroyer and did other extensive damage were OSA-Class Soviet vessels. India's new muscle probably serves effectively to deter any aggressive ideas the Chinese might have—if, indeed, they have such thoughts. India, on the other hand, could conceivably test its new strength in limited attempts to change the status quo in border areas. China would have to react, looking back apprehensively at the Soviet Union as it did so. Without active Soviet support for India, the PLA could cope. Part of the military threat now posed by India is its ability to join in multifront attacks on the PRC, or to invoke active Soviet support in what began as a bilateral conflict.

With mobile (or even merely moveable) nuclear weapons, the PRC can threaten most of India's territory from Tibet or other nearby points. India, in this sense, would occupy the same position with respect to the Soviet Union that Japan holds in United States strategy. Peking could make India a hostage, but would not dare to face the retaliation that would be provoked by first use. In order to field a credible Indian deterrent, New Delhi must undertake the production of fairly long-range missiles in order to reach vital industrial and population centers in China.

The smaller states bordering on China offer no military threat in themselves, although access to the mainland *via* these territories is a planning problem for the PLA. If unimpeded by the great powers, the PLA could invade and take over much of Southeast Asia, although the Chinese might be faced with hostile applications of their own people's war principles in some places. It is difficult, however, to imagine the circumstances that would encourage such action. There is no evidence that the PRC sees any threat from them that would evoke a preemptive attack. Equally, China does not covet their territory, although control over the political and economic policies of its neighbors certainly fits into the general concept of PRC hegemony in Asia.

No offshore Asian country offers any current threat to China except as it might lend its territory to use by others as bases for attack. Australia, the Philippines, and Indonesia have such a potential, and some United States activities in the first two may be seen as elements of a global United States strategic system that menaces China. In the material sense, there is little that the PRC can do about it; moreover, in actual conflict the PLA would have its hands full in trying to deal with threats closer to home.

We may conclude that, for the moment, China is preoccupied with the problem defined by a massive and threatening Soviet military presence along the border. The United States has the continuing capability to attack in great strength, particularly from sea and air. Japan is being watched carefully, but the visible military element of Tokyo's posture is, for the moment, of little significance. Other Asian nations threaten China only as allies or collaborators with the major powers. Preoccupied with a critical defense problem, China is steadily enhancing its overall ability to cope by developing modern forces which inevitably have significanct offensive power beyond the borders. In simple military logic, China cannot make a major attack on the Soviet Union or the United States with any hope of success. Neither can Peking attack their allies or other nations in whose security the two superpowers have a substantial interest.

6

Symmetries and Imbalances

It can be argued that the purely military characteristics of the PLA reflect a coherent view of the correct national strategy for China at this time, given its economic condition and the problems competing for the attention of the leadership. But one may then ask why the PRC, fearing the power of two major adversaries, has not done more to improve its defenses. Any attempt to answer this question involves speculation; but in the absence of any hard evidence, speculation may be useful.

It is entirely plausible that the correct mix of "people's war" and modernized forces has been the subject of serious conflict within the Chinese leadership. The group seeking rapid modernization has no doubt had to fight very hard for its programs, and has probably had to settle for less than it desired. Political and ideological sanctions have doubtless been invoked by all parties. But conceding all this, it may also be argued that the PRC has been fully aware of and

50

sensitive to a problem that has faced many governments: how to maintain maximum readiness within real physical constraints while making major changes in military posture. Institutional claims on limited resources provide the material for a continuing debate in Peking. If, in the interest of maintaining economic progress on a broad front, the central authorities have made the necessary constraining decisions about the PLA share, then an attempt to maintain readiness would involve the continuing assignment of significant defensive missions to the cheapest and largest Chinese resource—people. In effect, this style of defense not only embodies the Maoist revolutionary mystique; it also makes the best use of a military asset that finds its greatest role in homeland defense. It will have a real and important part to play in defense planning for some time to come.

But conventional formations with modern weapons are increasing in number and changing the total force "mix" in tactical doctrine. As noted earlier, the PLA has redefined some critical regional boundaries and moved forward some of its better-equipped strategic forces. The combination of more effective modern forces and regional boundary changes reflect planning for a defense in depth to give the regional commander uniform control over the approaches to the vital areas that he has to defend. Before the boundaries were redrawn, the commander in (for example) Peking had no responsibility in a zone that included the vital approaches to his command. These changes are no doubt a response to increasing Soviet pressure, but they also reflect the influence of a reassessment of the style of response of which the PLA in increasingly capable. The logic returns full circle to Mao's 1938 statement about modernization:[50]

> The reform of our military system requires its modernization and improved technical equipment, without which we cannot drive the enemy back across the Yalu River.

The PLA, as it stands today, testifies to a thoughtful application of available resources to a defined strategic problem:

---

[50] Mao Tse-tung, "On Protracted War," in *Selected Military Writings*, second edition (Peking: Foreign Languages Press, 1966), p. 259.

The PLA is now armed with a full range of conventional ground weapons, including artillery to which United States officials give high ratings. Curiously, there is little open evidence of interest in close air support of ground operations.

Tactical and logistical mobility have been increased by a significant rise in battlefield personnel carriers, trucks, and railroad mileage. The new capabilities are best suited to operations inside China; their usefulness would fall off somewhat beyond the borders.

Air defense has been upgraded by more and better aircraft, SAMs, and improved electronics. This is most apparent inside China, and there is little to indicate development of an extended expeditionary capability.

Inside China, the ability to attack an invader's bases and LOCs has been considerably enhanced by general improvements in aircraft and some growth in rocket strength. There is a shortage of aircraft able to attack at greater range beyond China, and the economics of battle would induce a conservative view of the expenditure of scarce nuclear weapons carriers in this role.

Modernization in naval forces has gone almost entirely to the improvement in close-in defenses. In this case, the PRC has shown some progress; but the PLA submarine would find it difficult to survive very long under modern antisubmarine warfare techniques if the Chinese should elect, for example, to try to close Japanese ports or operate at great distances from home.

As discussed earlier, the PRC nuclear weapons program suggests a conscious effort to keep open as many options as possible, remembering that some are already foreclosed by the nuclear power of the United States and Soviet Union. If the reports of recent increased emphasis on IRBMs is correct, this would reinforce the belief that defensive deterrence against the Soviet Union has high priority and is enhanced by the ability to strike deeper into metropolitan Russia. Meanwhile, the first ICBM test is yet to come.

A Balance

There is substantial symmetry between the forces in being in China (including also the general trend of improvement plans), and the hypothesis that Peking's primary concern is defense against attack on the homeland by the United States or the Soviet Union, with a principal focus now on the latter. Weaknesses in posture can be attributed to internal differences, or to lack of resources, or to inability to produce and absorb at any faster rate. It is probable that all three factors are involved.

If the PRC is deliberately contemplating sizeable and extended operations beyond its borders, then there are important imbalances and shortcomings in known preparations: force availability; air endurance and overseas air operations problems; inadequate naval capabilities; reduction in mobility and logistics capacity when beyond the Chinese railway system—to name only a few. Both positive and negative factors support the argument that the PLA is, first and foremost, a defensive force.

Important Reservations

It is not argued here that China is essentially peaceloving and passive. Limits on action are set by a host of conditions, among which overall priorities and physical inhibitions loom large. There are two great cliches that, despite a certain triteness, must be considered in any assessment of the usefulness of PLA forces. However modest its immediate goals, and however circumspect its present actions, China's total view of itself as a great power includes the concept of a rightful hegemony in Asia. If no effective opposition, present or prospective, were in view, Peking would be greatly tempted to assert its position by the simplest means of all—military domination. The presence of a vacuum in Asia would create an unstable situation.

Second, there is the cliche about the indifference of the gun. It is not concerned about whom it shoots. It is conceivable that continuing improvement in PLA combat capabilities, for whatever initial purposes, might tempt the Chinese leaders to tests of strength or military adventures that they earlier would have avoided. Whatever the present odds against such an eventuality, other powers cannot avoid pondering its implications for their future strategy in Asia.

7

Implications for Strategic Developments in Asia

How does the PLA as a fighting force enter into the projection of future military strategies and postures in Asia? China cannot now, or at any time in the reasonably foreseeable future, "get at" the United States directly. If and when Peking fields an ICBM force, it will at first be a second-strike, countervalue force. In simple terms, this would alter the balance of deterrence, but not in the sense of a Chinese first strike capability as an immediate factor. Indirect deterrence, focused on United States allies such as Japan or the Republic of Korea as hostages, is a much more real and immediate consideration. The only course open to the United States seems to be the maintenance of the capability and will to retaliate against mainland China should it initiate the use of nuclear weapons. China has repeatedly pledged "no first use," and its vulnerability to counterstrikes is at least one of the reasons for this. Conversely, the United States is inhibited by the Chinese ability to do serious damage to its allies, particularly Japan.

Hsieh speculates[51] on China's interest in tactical nuclear weapons delivered by aircraft, which would be particularly useful in homeland defense, but also in places like Korea, where the terrain imposes strict requirements for accuracy of delivery. In a defensive situation, it is conceivable that both sides might feel some restraint on the use of larger strategic weapons.

The spectrum of nuclear possibilities for the PRC, while constrained by technical and resource problems, is nevertheless significant. Properly managed, it can produce a large payoff for a limited investment. There is not yet enough evidence to support any firm conclusions about the direction of Chinese programs. For the present, it appears that Peking is preoccupied with some sort of interim response to the pressures it feels from the Soviet Union. Over the short haul, this should temper United States concerns; but an accelerated and enlarged production will eventually generate a potential that must figure significantly in United States estimates of PRC capabilities.

The great powers need do little more than they are now doing to oppose Chinese airborne or amphibious operations. The thinness of PLA resources for these special forms of war would only permit small-scale efforts that could be largely contained by local forces, with some outside air and naval help. In the absence of this support, the PRC might be able to offset qualitative deficiencies by the massive use of more primitive means.

India is now building Mig-21 aircraft and good tanks in its own factories, and New Delhi also feels that it can count on effective support from Moscow in an emergency. Hence, the United States should have little concern over the prospect of a major PRC attack against India. PLA forces, if unopposed, could intimidate (and, if necessary, invade) a number of smaller neighboring countries. But there are two powerful deterrents to any such ventures: Soviet deployments and United States capabilities. China would have to feel desper-

---

[51] *China's Nuclear Strategy and a United States Anti-China ABM*, Statement before the Subcommittee on Arms Control, International Law and Organization, Foreign Relations Committee, United States Senate, April 9, 1970, p. 12.

ate indeed to send forces beyond its borders in the face of these conditions.

The general military equation in Asia has some dangerous instabilities, most particularly in the Sino-Soviet situation. There is little the United States can do to use its military power to influence this relationship. The best hope of all parties is mutual restraint short of major hostilities. Meanwhile, however the Nixon Doctrine may operate in practice, the United States must make it continually clear that it would be very risky to extend the Sino-Soviet rivalry to third countries in Asia simply because the United States appears to be reducing its physical presence.

It would be misleading to suggest that the military forces of the PRC today represent any ideal condition. The differences between PLA weaponry, on the one hand, and either United States or Soviet equipment on the other, are too great to induce any complacency in Peking. The time needed and the resources involved in any attempt to reach parity with the superpowers make any such aspiration a virtually impossible dream. Recognizing this reality, the Chinese leadership has made some basic decisions relating to perceived threat priorities and resource availability. Whether consciously or not, Peking has achieved, and is improving, a general force posture that is directed most particularly to the defense of the realm against the looming threat of the Soviet Union. How real this threat is may be debatable; but there is a temptation to conclude that Peking is best prepared to fight the type of war that focuses on defense against the Soviet Army, and that is least likely to be engaged in by the United States. If this interpretation is correct, then it follows that the effort has been to achieve a posture that has steadily raised the cost of an attack on China. Any major test of Peking's ability to defend its territory would involve tremendous damage to China; but the attacker would also have to think seriously about the costs and the level of damage that he or his allies would suffer in the process. In contrast, while the use of the PLA in something other than defense is, in the purely physical sense, entirely possible, the military balance at the present time provides a powerful disincentive against such employment.

Selected Bibliography

George, Alexander L. *The Chinese Communist Army in Action* (New York and London: Columbia University Press, 1967).

Gelber, Harry C. "The Impact of Chinese ICBM's on Strategic Deterrence," *Orbis* (Summer 1969).

Gittings, John. *The Role of the Chinese Army* (London: Oxford University Press, 1967).

Griffith, Samuel B. II. *The Chinese People's Liberation Army* (New York: McGraw-Hill, 1967).

Harding, Harry, Jr. "The Making of Chinese Military Policy," in Whitson, William W. (editor), *The Military and Political Power in China in the 1970's* (New York: Praeger, 1972).

Hinton, Harold C. *The Bear at the Gate* (American Enterprise Institute for Public Policy Research and Hoover Institution on War, Revolution and Peace, 1971).

————. *China's Turbulent Quest*, revised edition (Bloomington and London: Indiana University Press, 1972).

Hsieh, Alice Langley. "China's Nuclear Missile Programme: Regional or Intercontinental?" *China Quarterly* (January-March 1971).

Joffe, Ellis. *Party and Army: Professional and Political Control in the Chinese Officer Corps* (Cambridge: Harvard University Press, 1967).

Liu Chi-pu. *A Military History of Modern China* (Princeton: Princeton University Press, 1956).

Mao Tse-tung. *Selected Military Writings*, second edition (Peking: Foreign Languages Press, 1966).

Maxwell, Neville. *India's China War* (Garden City: Doubleday, 1972).

Nelsen, Harvey. "Military Forces in the Cultural Revolution," *China Quarterly* (July-September 1972).

Powell, Ralph L. "Maoist Military Doctrines," *Asian Survey* (April 1968).

Stark, John R. (director). *People's Republic of China: An Economic Assessment* (Washington: Joint Economic Committee, US Congress, 1972).

Trager, Frank N., and Henderson, William (editors). *Communist China, 1949–1969, A Twenty-Year Appraisal* (New York: New York University Press, 1971).

National Strategy Information Center, Inc.

Strategy Papers

Edited by Frank N. Trager and William Henderson
With the assistance of Dorothy E. Nicolosi

The People's Liberation Army: Communist China's Armed Forces by Angus M. Fraser. October 1973.

Nuclear Weapons and the Atlantic Alliance by Wynfred Joshua, May 1973

How to Think About Arms Control and Disarmament by James E. Dougherty, August 1973.

The Military Indoctrination of Soviet Youth by Leon Gouré, January 1973

The Asian Alliance: Japan and United States Policy by Franz Michael and Gaston J. Sigur, October 1972

Iran, The Arabian Peninsula, and the Indian Ocean by R. M. Burrell and Alvin J. Cottrell, September 1972

Soviet Naval Power: Challenge for the 1970s by Norman Polmar, April 1972

How Can We Negotiate with the Communists? by Gerald L. Steibel, March 1972